The Lord Jesus Healed Me

The Journey of an Atheist to the Truth

TONY MYERS

© Copyright 2016 Tony Myers
ISBN-13: 9781540789655
ISBN-10: 1540789659
Library of Congress Control Number: 2016920576
CreateSpace Independent Publishing Platform
North Charleston, South Carolina

EDITED BY: DIANA JAMERSON
COVER BY: JOHN JAMERSON, REFRESHED SITES

TABLE OF CONTENTS

ACKNOWLEDGEMENTS

Hello, this book is written to instill hope, where there may not be any hope to be seen. The Lord Jesus is no respecter people. What He did for me, He will do for you. Never give up; never lose Hope!! This is my journey. Please be encouraged from it: BE Healed In Jesus Name! This book took four years, for me to gather up the courage,   to write. I want to dedicate this book to Our Heavenly Father and to My Lord Jesus, without whom I wouldn't be here! Also, to my beloved wife (Deb) for loyally standing firm in her faith, throughout our whole marriage. A heartfelt thank-you goes out to the ones who encouraged me to write this book. John and Diana Jamerson, thanks for all of your help and encouragement, without whom this would not have been accomplished. Hey, readers if you need to build a web-site, check out Refreshed Sites, John and Diana are awesome! Joyce Rice Jacobs, thank you so much for your encouragement, for all the time you spent reading my drafts, and for your input. To anyone I've forgotten, thanks! God Bless and be encouraged!

FOREWORD

Written By Yvonne Miracle Webb

I can't recall the date or year that I met Tony and Deb but I do remember and will not forget the day he was healed. I worked at the church Tony and Deb attended at the time. When I first met Tony he was walking. He kept getting worse and doctors really didn't know what was causing it. The doctors were saying MS, then Lou Gherigs Disease, then an unknown neurological disease. He eventually started to come to church in a wheel chair. He was even baptized in a wheel chair. His health kept deteriorating. I would notice that he was missing church service more and more. I would call and check on him and ask him if he wanted the church van to pick him up for service since he wasn't able to drive anymore and Deb was not physically able to lift him.

All the while Tony was still attending church when he could. There is one moment in church that still stands out so vividly and powerfully to me. We were in praise and worship and I remember being tired and being reluctant to stand. My eyes caught Tony, he being unable to stand, lifting his body up with his weaken arms and holding himself up at a walker so that he could stand and worship our Lord, his Lord! I will never forget that. What an inspiration!!!!

My daughter had a worship team practice early on July 4th for an Fourth of July concert taking place in the parking lot of a local shopping center. I debated back & forth on whether to stay with her or go to the office with my husband. I just couldn't decide. I finally chose to stay at the practice. I was sitting and talking to a friend I hadn't seen in a while when I saw Deb walking from around some parked cars. She had a very odd look about her. I jumped up and walk towards her. I then saw Tony walking and pushing his wheelchair toward me. I couldn't believe my eyes! I remember excitingly getting the attention of others around me to notice Tony.

What rejoicing! Texts and Facebook videos being posted. Tony walking without any assistance and giving his testimony of praying for himself at home early that day. He stopped and talked to anyone he saw in a wheelchair. He even pick up his wheel chair and place in the back of his vehicle.

It was very hot that day and everyone was getting concerned that Tony was going to get overheated waiting on the concert. My family had the privilege of taking him and Deb to Cracker Barrel. God had placed this in my heart months ago put the timing was never right. Now was the right time. God's time. We sat and stared at him while he ate country fried steak. We even videotaped him. He wasn't supposed to be able to swallow. He ate the whole thing. As the time past that day you could see Tony getting stronger and stronger. As weeks and months pass Tony continue to amaze his physical therapist and doctors. He went off all his medication cold turkey without any complications. Who does that? Those who are healed of our LORD! Thank you Lord for allowing me to witness Tony's healing on July fourth 2012.
Yvonne Webb.

1

It was a dark and stormy night and the wind was howling.... oops!!! That's not how this story starts.

This is the story of my healing. For those who are not aware, on July 4, 2012, I was healed of Lou Gherig's disease/unknown neurological disorder, and several other health issues. In order for you to really understand that this Blessing I received is available for all, there is a true need for me to share some of my life story with you. This will show what a messed up individual I was, and how no matter where you are at in life, salvation is available. Healing is available, and a life restored to its fullest potential, is available to all.

Here is a glimpse into my former life and my testimony of Christ. Sit back with a cup of pure black coffee, and let your understanding abound! A baby boy was born to a young Catholic couple in New Haven, IN, and Lord they didn't know what they were in for! The second born out of four children, and the oldest boy out of two. We were an athletic family with the main sports being swimming and tennis. My earliest memories are participating in these sports. My parents provided us with a safe and stable environment, which is evident when you look at my sisters and brother. They have all have led stable lives, minus one; me! I did partake in the family sports, but secretly I was also learning the world of lying, drinking and drugs.

My father, who wasn't a heavy drinker, kept cases of wine in the basement, and there would be a six pack of beer in the refrigerator. So, little Tony at the age of eight would sneak drinks from the bottle of wine, and also from the beer in the refrigerator. I would go so far as to mark the bottle of beer, being extremely careful not to drink an amount that would be noticed. I also found cigarettes and coffee right, around this same time. My grandmother smoked, so I would steal packs of cigarettes from her, when we would visit her. From that time period on, I would steal cigarettes from others that smoked, such was my early life.

We attended a Catholic church every Sunday or Saturday night. Here, I would hear people make fun of others, who were not dressed in the proper attire. I thought to myself, "So this is how God talks, about those who don't meet up to His Standards." I do remember hearing about Jesus, but most, of what I remember is trying to meet the high standards God expected from us. If you didn't meet them, He would discard you to the bowels of the earth otherwise known as Hell.

One day I was taking a bath, when suddenly a man appeared in the bathroom. I knew it was Jesus, because there was brightness all around Him, and He appeared much like, what I had imagined He would. His features were harsh, and He had His arms spread, and didn't say a word. To my thinking, He didn't say a word to me, because He was ashamed of me, and didn't want anything to do with me. I told my mother and sister about this, and my sister responded with "What would Jesus want to do with a naked boy like you?" Which confirmed to me what I thought, Jesus had judged me, and I didn't live up to His standards. It was at this point that I determined, if Jesus didn't want anything to do with me I wouldn't have anything to do with Him.

The rest of my young years can be summed up with one word: rebellion. By the time I attended junior high school and high school, I started calling myself the preacher of death and destruction. I had teachers and friends, who tried to speak good into my life, but I wouldn't have anything to do with it. In junior high school, two of my friends died. Both deaths had drugs and drinking involved; and one of which, I did blame on myself. We had gotten into a fistfight at school, and I told him what I thought of him. That evening, he was decapitated in a car wreck. God was punishing me!

Let me interject a thought here, the time line of all this escapes me, but I'm just trying to give an overview of my thought processes at the time. At one point, I attempted to kill myself, and was put into a program to get me straightened out. It was shortly after that, I left home of my own choice. I did manage to graduate high school while living on my own. I lived from place to place, and stayed with those who were like minded. Drinking and drugs were my end all objective, along with taking out my anger on those, who would mention Jesus or God. At the young age of 17, I found myself working at McDonald's as a maintenance man. I was dating a college girl, and she became pregnant. She decided to have an abortion, which completely angered me. I had no clue what to do, so it was off to the military I went.

Military life suited my life-style, and I spent a total of eight years in the military. I was actually a good soldier, was respected for my on-duty performance, and received commendations and awards. Off-duty performance, I was a complete disaster, though none of the charges ever stuck to me. I was probably awarded the most restrictions ever, but never received a court martial, or even given full-blown Article Fifteen, although I was given many summarized Article Fifteen's. Even while I was on restriction, especially when I was stationed overseas, I would end up in trouble. Some of my exploits were: swimming in the Panama Canal during a time of conflict in a highly secured area, and fighting against fourteen other soldiers. That didn't go too well for me. In summary, if you can imagine it, I probably did it. I was sent to the Army's In-Hospital Drug and Alcohol Treatment Center twice. Those of you, who are familiar with it, you know at that time most soldiers, who are sent there, are discharged and going through that treatment, so they can be prepared for civilian life. They kept me in, and I received an honorable discharge in 1995. I'm not going into great detail here, because I only want to give an overview of how I used to live my life, but do not want it to overshadow the life changing miracle that was to come. How's that cup of coffee? Mine is good!

This book is about instilling Hope, (confidant expectation) and no matter how far you've gone, it's one step up to the bright shining light of Jesus! Unfortunately, I still had a long way to fall, before I chose that step! Once I was honorably discharged, it was as if the leash was taken off. My age was around twenty-seven, and various jobs came and went. Everything from selling Kirby Vacuum cleaners to carpentry. Then I found welding. Despite my lifestyle of drinking and drugs, my reliability, no matter the job, was remarkable. Also well-known was who to contact if you needed a fix. The city was Phenix City, in Alabama.

When I left the military, as far as I was concerned, life, was only about surviving until death; which in my thoughts would hopefully come quickly. My problem was I had no hope. The whole world seemed dark even in the brightest sunlight. If I wasn't drunk or high, my constant state was: panic, depression, and paranoia; later to be diagnosed as PTSD. When I was sober, I couldn't stand to be in a lighted room, or around windows. I was good at disguising this, which is why I stayed drunk. Honestly, my plan was to be dead before the age of 35. I had long hair, wore a bandana. and had an earring in my left ear. The earrings were always long and ob-noxious. This is so funny to me now! My street name was Gypsy Man, and only employers knew my real name. Everyone else called me Gypsy. I'm sure you've noticed that God wasn't anywhere in the picture, and few people dared to talk to me about God or Jesus. The ones, who were brave enough to approach me, ended up with a sound cussing out, or worse yet, being jumped on. So now you get the picture that "Mr. Nice Guy" didn't describe me at this point. I was the type of person that normal people would avoid, although there were some people, that I did become friends with; and I do credit these people with giving me some sense of sanity. They know who they are, and I thank them from the bottom of my heart.

Even though I hated God, and said He didn't exist, He was still there. Retrospectively, he had a great part in keeping me alive. Times when I should have been shot, stabbed, or killed in a car wreck. Something would always happen, and I would survive. One time, at two o'clock in the morning, coming out from a bar and crossing the street, a car came, out of nowhere, headed straight for me. I honestly do not know if it actually hit me. I was lifted high up into the air, but not thrown! The reason I say this is, because I landed softly about fifty feet from where I was, and evidently the driver also thought he had hit me. He was a young man in his early twenties, and he was terrified. I told him I was fine, and he could leave. I then walked, about ten miles home. Thank you Jesus! Another time I was driving down a country road at a breakneck speed on a hairpin curve, and the car ended up in the ditch totaled. The driver and myself walked away from it, and yes drinking was involved. Okay, enough of that, but I do need to tell you that at this point in my life, I had not paid or filed taxes since 1995. My driver's license had been suspended, and I had been to jail more than once. Not a nice person! Have you gotten a clear picture of who I USED to be? Good, let's make a pot of coffee, and get to what you want to hear about!!

This book is about HOPE and INSPIRATION, and how awesomely GOOD The Father and Jesus are. He has brought me out of all of this, and more! No matter the situation you find yourself in. Whether it's yourself or a loved one, that may be living like I was or worse, the Father wants a changed life. Whether it's: drugs, alcohol, a terrible financial situation, mental illness or a deadly disease, our Loving Father wants to correct it, but He needs our willingness to do so, and our cooperation!

2

The year is 2006, the state of my life is that I owe the IRS over 35,000 dollars, my driver's license has been suspended since 1996, I had been in jail, and was hopelessly drunk. My drug use was now a little sporadic, and my mental condition was still a mess. I had depression, anger, fear, and an unstable mind. Little did I know, change was coming and rather quickly. The change that came was: good, bad, ugly, and uglier. Then so mind blowing awesome, that a movie writer couldn't imagine it. How's your coffee holding up? My wife just made me a pot. Yes, that is a diversionary tactic.

This next part truly makes me nervous. How much should I include? What parts should I leave out? This story is about hope. Creating hope in people, no matter how bad the situation is. In order to reach those people who might be in a similar situation as I was, I needed to add a portion, that very honestly I would prefer not to talk about. Yet, it is a large part of the story, and in order to fully understand what an awesome miracle my healing is, you must know the whole story. Aha! Right now you're thinking "What is it?!!" Okay, here we go, in the world, everything is not perfect. Meaning being a veteran, and the present civilian support of our veterans. I don't want my treatment, by the medical people, to overshadow how good The Father and Jesus are. The lack of medical treatment is a part of my story, but I must tell it to encourage those, who may right now be experiencing this. Jesus is not dependent on medicine, and He can do wondrous things in spite of man's lack of ability.

In 2006, with the realization that massive change was needed in my life, I enrolled in an online college program. Me, the guy who had never touched a computer, had actually refused to do so, was also the person, who had disdain for school and education. At thirty-nine years old, I entered higher education, and enrolled to get an Associate's Degree in Information Technology. I hadn't even touched a computer up to this point, nor had I ever been on the Internet. The first thing, that changed, was that the drugs had to go, and in a large part, they did. My drinking also slowed down, and although there were still binges, nowhere near the case of beer a day, and large amounts of liquor that had been my normal. This is one thing that Hope does. Without hope there is only misery, but with Hope there is life! What followed was two years of nose to the grindstone, hoping to make a better life for myself. Two important things happened during this time. I met the woman who would later introduce me to Christ, and who stood by me through the most horrible time of my life. The other was the onset of symptoms, and in retrospect, this was largely, because I ignored the symptoms the best I could.

I was working, as a welder, in a company that produced trailers. Often times I would get severely tired, beyond normal, and have a headache that would become ruthless at times. Along with having a complete lack of appetite, which I ignored as well. Let's back-up a couple of sentences, so I can introduce you to the woman of my life! Her name was Debra Young. Now, as of 2011, it is Debra Myers. Please. If you meet her, don't call her Debra. Call her Debbie. Thanks, I appreciate that small act of kindness! We met through a game site online called Pogo, which was a site I went to when my college homework had me frustrated, and that happened often! I joined a league, that she was on. And That is the proverbial, That! She lived in Virginia, and I lived in Phenix City, AL. So in our minds, the chance of our actually ever meeting, was pretty close to none. We became friends, and talked almost every day, because she was a retired school teacher. She would proofread my college essays for me. Here's the twist, she told me she was a Christian, which figuring we'd never meet anyways, seemed OK with me, as long as she didn't shove Jesus down my throat. I didn't tell her I was an atheist, but simply said "Me and God have problems with each other". In 2008, my college degree was earned with a GPA of 3.71. Not bad for someone, who hadn't used their brain in some 40 years!

We continued our friendship. Then in October 2008, while we were talking in the chat room at the game site, another person chimed in saying "We must be sitting next to other." We laughed, and said no. We were simply friends and lived states away from each other. That sparked something in us, we talked about it, and realized that we had indeed fallen in love! We then hatched a crazy plan. I was going to leave Alabama, and move to Virginia. I don't believe it was so crazy on my part. I had nothing to lose, and everything to gain. I gave my two week's notice, and on November 13, 2008 headed to Virginia! This was a brand-new start for me. A new life where no one knew me, except for Deb. I must point out that, amazingly enough, I had been almost completely honest with her, except my having been hospitalized for drugs and alcohol. She knew I drank, but didn't know how much I had struggled with alcoholism; or the atheist thing. I did tell her not to even mention church. She could go all she wanted, but leave me out of it. She made it quite clear that getting drunk would not be tolerated. Did I mention she is a strong woman!

I arrived in Harrogate, TN at the Exxon Gas Station. Here's a funny side-note. On my trip there, I had actually gotten lost in Morristown, TN. I kept asking people where Harrogate, TN, was and no one knew. Deb, quickly figured out, that this was because I kept mispronouncing it. Saying Harrowell, or something similar. I had called her to ask, if she could give me directions, she couldn't because I could not tell her exactly where I was. I just kept blindly driving, and did eventually find Harrogate at 4 am in the morning. Another little nugget about me is that I get lost in cities, even with a GPS. Honestly! Put me in the desert, a swamp or jungle, and I can navigate. If you put me on a street with a vehicle, getting lost is what I'm doing.

Deb, Brandy (Deb's Sheltie) and myself were a match made in heaven, except for my cussing, Deb was not used to it, especially the GD word.

She asked me not to say it, and I did my best. On the property, there was a cave, I enjoyed going down into it, I loved it. On my first trip down, a bobcat appeared. I love animals, and always felt more at home with animals than with people. I managed to get within four feet of it, and just talk to it. Every time I would go down there, the bobcat was there, and I would sit and talk to it. After my healing, I went down to the cave, and there was no sign of it.

Another area of difficulty was finding a job. In a small town, where everyone knows everyone. When a stranger comes in, it is not the most welcoming situation. I even tried being a substitute teacher. One of the requirements was to have a principal in that school district recommend you with a Letter of Recommendation. I went around to the schools and talked with many principles. I finally found one, who said that a letter would be written. With that done, the school called me in to substitute a high school computer class. It went fantastic, the regular class teacher was quite happy. However, the woman who was in charge of substitute teachers called, and told us that what we thought was a letter of recommendation, turned out to be a letter not recommending me. It was a letter telling them that I couldn't be recommended; because of the fact that I hadn't lived in the area for long. The school then let me know that they were unable to use me anymore.

3

A point I need to make clear is, at this time, the change in myself had started to happen, back when I was in college. My rough edges were softened some, but by most people's standards there was a long way to go. One thing was the very apparent love of Christ in Deb. When we traveled to Knoxville, she would often give panhandlers a five dollar bill or whatever change she had. This appalled me, and after chewing her out, I would inform her that most panhandlers have tons of money. This wouldn't make a difference. She would still do it. It was her caring for others that really started a change in me.

In January 2009, my job search ended with me finding work as a welder for a company that made dump trailers. At this point, my back had started to hurt fairly relentlessly. It did not hamper me, having a high tolerance for pain. Three months went by I, found fulfillment in having a job, and enjoying working again! Meanwhile, I pursued my Bachelor's Degree in Business Information, which was hampered some by an unreliable internet provider. Nevertheless, with Deb's continual encouragement, this area of my life was moving forward as well. With Deb's help and encouragement, with sometimes a somewhat stern voice, we pursued, and did get my driver's license. That had been suspended for 14 years. We also continued paying on my back taxes, and things were looking up!

Around March, one day I was at work holding a piece of steel, while my welding partner, was tacking it in place. My legs and arms suddenly got weak, and the heavy piece of steel plating was dropped. If my partner had not been extremely fast, it would have crushed his head. He was decent about it, but the sudden realization that I had put his life in jeopardy hit me hard. After talking to the supervisor, I decided to call it a day. Weeks prior to that, a doctor's appointment had been made to find out, what was going on with my back. It had taken Deb, and her niece, alot of urging to convince me to make the appointment. I had a problem, so let's call it for what it was: a hatred for the medical field and doctors in particular! I wouldn't go to them. Every time I had been severely cut before, I had always stitched myself up. Except for one time, I had been hit on the back of the head with a tire iron.

That appointment was for the next day, which I informed my supervisor and plant manager. The next day, I was off to the VA Medical Center, ugh, grrrrrrr and phtttttt! Needless to say, that would be the first of many frustrating trips to the doctor, and my blood pressure would skyrocket the moment I entered the building. As I recall, tests were ordered, or done at the facility. An interesting anecdote, on the way home from a trip to the emergency room, something happened that has always stuck with both myself and Deb. It was a two hour trip from the VA to home. Once, during a rain storm, it was very hard to see the road, when all of sudden a cross appeared that said "Prepare to meet God". I went "off" saying "Why in the world would anyone put a sign like that out there? Didn't they know that could cause and accident?!" I guess you could say, that the sign caused fear in me. It was after my healing, that Deb and I would laugh about that incident. She would make fun of me for it! Another time, on another trip to the emergency room. Deb had to call her nephew, and my parents, to get me to go. She said that my skin color was so disturbing: a bluish red. I felt as if an elephant was on my chest. On the way home we experienced my first real snowstorm in years, and we couldn't even see the road. After that first doctor's appointment, I went back to work only to find out, that they had already replaced me. The plant manager explained that they had realized how severe my condition was, and they could not wait around to replace me. They let me know that if the doctors were able to fix me, then a job would be waiting for me.

Jobless again. It was frustrating to go from being physically fit and unstoppable, to being in constant pain. The back pain got so severe that I did take the pain medicine, which would not really help. It was probably because of my history with drugs, which I was not doing anymore. My drinking at this time was fairly rare as well, because I didn't want to destroy my relationship with Deb. Without a job, but recognizing the need to try to stay active, I commenced clearing the field that had once been a tobacco field of Deb's parents. It was getting harder and harder, for me to lift my feet up to even get on the riding lawn mower, which was becoming more and more difficult very quickly. My symptoms were piling up. Now my breathing was labored. and I would get dizzy. The constant headache was becoming more and more painful, and constant. My legs would suddenly just collapse, and I would end up on the ground.

This time would've been around August of 2009. There were two or so more doctors visits, where the doctor would say "Tony you're doing better", which was anything but the truth. Deb told him that I needed assistance walking, and that I would fall often. An appointment was made for me to get assistance with that (a cane), for six months down the road. Deb was furious, with how long this was going to take, but I was too. It was then that I decided to make my own cane, to give me something to do. The headaches had made pursuing my college degree very difficult, because I couldn't concentrate. So rather than sitting around all day doing nothing, I took to whittling a cane, and enjoyed it. I learned how to carve and preserve canes on the internet, after I made the first cane. Now I was using that cane, which was a struggle because by this time a walker was actually needed. I was using the cane almost like a walker. DISCLAMER: Deb and I are terrible with dates, so the time-periods here are to the best of our recollection. The results from the "so-called tests" showed disc-deterioration and other things. An appointment with a surgeon was scheduled for months down the road, and in the meantime they gave me one round of a spinal injection. Something weird happened. So with that and the increasing symptoms, the recommendation was no more injections. That totally went with my philosophy, of not having anything to do with doctors.

4

You may be wondering "Where was Jesus in all of this?" Deb, being a Holy Spirit filled Christian, did not push Him on me. Occasionally, I would go into the bedroom, see her watching some preacher on TV, that I would make fun of, and do a hilarious impersonation of. Deb would have to laugh. Then one day one of us, and we disagree who mentioned it first. Deb says she did, but I said I did, mentioned going to church. Regardless, guess who agreed to go? Yes, I did. I do not even know what was going on in my mind at this time, as to why I agreed to that idea. Although, I did inform Deb that there was going to be no dressing up garbage. It was my typical outfit: torn jeans and my flannel shirt. If so much as one person looked cross-eyed at me, that person would be assaulted, and I would never enter another church again.

I had no idea what to expect. Maybe I was expecting the church building to fall on top of me. Deb took me to a church her nephew had recommended to her years before. As we walked into the church, I was so uncomfortable, and had no idea what to expect. Other than Deb, the other Christians I had been involved with, were always very condemning. The very first person, that I saw was a fella with a bandana on with faded jeans. I thought "Okay, now this is cool, this place may be all right." There was a relatively young preacher, who started preaching, and even the music was pretty good. We sat in the back row. A few people came up, and shook our hands. I do remember a few people calling me Brother, and I thought "What in the world is up with that?" The thought came to me, " I ain't your brother!" I wanted to say it out loud, but all of the sudden Deb looked at me, as if she knew my thoughts. The words that the preacher said did not have an impact on me as I can recall, but then again I was having a severe headache, along with a constant back pain. I was trying to stand without falling, which made it hard to focus, throwing off my concentration. Afterwords, Deb asked what I thought, and I replied that it was okay.

How's your coffee holding up, do you need another pot, yet? Before that, here's an anecdote. I believe this happened on our next visit to the church, when I was using a walker. A woman walked up to me, and asked if she could pray for me. I said, "Okay, whatever", and she started speaking crazy. She wasn't speaking English or any other type of language that I understood. We're standing there in the parking lot, and here is this crazy woman, with her hand on my shoulder speaking weird! I backed up so she would get her hands off of me, but she went on for two or three minutes. I had no clue what she was doing. A small piece of advice here, never walk up to someone you don't know, and start speaking in tongues! I remember seeing Deb wondering what I thought of it, and if I'd ever want to go back to that church again. When we got in the car, I asked her "What in the world was that all about?" She told me that it was a type of praying, but I just thought it was crazy! Funny thing today, speaking in tongues, is the majority of my prayer life. Okay, let's get us some good hot, pure black coffee! Nothing like a good hot cup of coffee, warming up the insides of a body!

5

By the end of 2009, I had seen the doctor about three times, and each time my symptoms had multiplied. There had been a CT scan, MRI's, and an EMG. Half of these performed there, and the other half we had to drive in to West Virginia. I had many visits to the emergency room, where they would recommend, and set up appointments for "this or that test". Most of which were canceled, presumably by the primary care physician. The days that we did see the doctor, it was "Mr. Myers you look a lot better." They continued to say this, even though my condition was becoming worse, and the symptoms were growing in number. The last time we saw a doctor, my wife told him that I was falling down often while using the cane and she felt a walker was needed. I must be honest, that the way I feel about doctors, I really did not list all of the symptoms I was having, but my wife would tell the doctor most of the symptoms. Another appointment was made with the prosthetic department for months down the road, and when we went to that appointment, they ended up giving me a walker with small wheels that I couldn't even navigate to the car. Seriously, it wouldn't even go over the small cracks in the parking lot, and I ended up falling. By this time, I was using my upper body strength for most things and would swing my legs forward, to move forward. The way I was getting around did not resemble walking at all. The speed, that I could walk, was ten feet in about ten minutes. We had actually already bought an appropriate walker, because it had taken so long to get an appointment. After this, Deb was convinced that we needed to try a different doctor in order to get something done.

This was around December 2009, and nothing had yet to be determined except for the back condition. The other symptoms were not discussed, or being looked into including my extreme lack of appetite. My stomach felt as if there were rocks in it, and I felt full all the time. I did, however, force myself to eat small amounts of food. I was still making the walking canes to pass the time, and even that was becoming more and more difficult and painful, with my fingers becoming harder to move. By this time, I had made about five canes, but even getting into the area where I made the canes was very difficult. This spot was a cellar under Deb's family house. Since it was winter, we had moved my tools down there, and that is where I worked. I loved it. I listened to the likes of: Ozzy Osbourne, Twisted Sister, AC/DC; all heavy metal bands! The way, that I got into the cellar was by crawling with great difficulty, but I found so much enjoyment in the chance for me to escape my woes. The only downside once again was my physical limitations. I also kept cutting myself, because of the lack of control and strength in my hands and fingers. On a certain occasion the carving knife slipped, and there was a deep gash in my hand that bled profusely. I tried to get the bleeding to stop, but it wouldn't. So I wrapped it in a towel, and started to make my way to the house. It was a very slow journey, although our trailer is only about 50 feet from the family house. By the time I got there, the blood had saturated the towel. I showed Deb, and she wasn't happy with me at all. With my aversion to doctors, there was no way I was going to see one. So I turned around, and used some glue, that held! That was the last time I would be going down to work on the canes.

6

The year of 2010 would prove to be a tough year, but then again so would 2011. I'm brewing a nice hot pot of coffee and I hope you're enjoying yours. It was pretty evident that my condition was not going to be a temporary thing, and we needed a source of income. We filed for my disability. Another development was that we had decided to switch VA hospitals and doctors, since very little was being done to help me. This was the year that there would be very few doctor visits, I was informed they wouldn't switch primary care doctor, unless I stopped seeing the doctor I was with. It would not be until January 2011, that the VA would set up an appointment. In 2010, the majority of doctor visits would be to the emergency room, where they actually did more for me than the primary doctor did. They set me up with an appointment for a sleep study test, and provided me with a breathing machine for sleep apnea, which I loathed. I was choking often now, so they also did a test for that. That brings us up-to date on the medical side of things.

On the church side, we attended that church often. On one occasion, at Deb's encouragement, we went to talk to the Pastor, He wasn't available, but we made an appointment to see him. The Business Manager asked if she could do anything to help, and Deb told her, that I was not a believer, and that she just wanted someone to talk with me. I remember her hollering for an old man who came in, and I told him that I was not so sure about this God business. He then started to pray for me saying out loud "I claim Tony as a fellow brother In Christ". I told him, "We'll see." What struck me was how presumptuous that encounter was, and I thought to myself "We'll just see about that!" I do give that fella credit for being so bold. The following week we had our appointment with the pastor, which we did keep. We talked more about the military and my health condition, than about God. This was around springtime of 2010, and Deb remembers how during this meeting, I kept choking on my saliva, and how both of them were terrified that I would stop breathing. I liked that fella, because he seemed down-to-earth, not the condemning type. Although the pain, in my back, really kept me from concentrating on what was actually said. One thing that came out of the discussion, was a VA Medical Center, that was in a different city than the one we were going to. It was at this time that Deb and I decided I should switch, although it would be over a year before an appointment would be made.

Myself being new to the area, I hadn't made any friends to speak of; nor was I up to visiting people anyway, Riding in a vehicle caused so much pain and discomfort. For the most part, our days were spent on the Pogo game site. We went to church a few times, during this time period, but most of the time I was in too much pain to be interested in going.

Neither my wife or I remember much from this time-period, our main goal was just "Hanging On", until we would go to see a new general practitioner. My condition was at the point, where in order to get up the steps to our trailer, I'd have to sit down on the steps, and scoot up each one using my arms. It was at this point, sometime in the fall of 2010, that once again we made another trip to the emergency room. This was at a different VA Medical Center. On the way to the hospital, (a three hour trip) I had to stop at a gas station to relieve myself. Deb dropped me off at the front of the store, and went to go park the car. I took a fall, and couldn't get back up. This happened right in front of the cashier window. The cashier saw me on the ground, and laughed. Roughly, eight people walked by, and not one person stopped to see if they could help. Along with everything else going on in my life at that time, this was a huge blow to my ego. I should also mention that, at this point, I was having extreme difficulty relieving myself, and was in constant pain.

It was. during this ER visit, Deb told them I needed a wheelchair to get around. She was doing the caring and loving thing by telling them how hard even taking a shower or bath was for me along with reaching things. Several times (more often than I could count) I had fallen and been unable to get back up. She, on different occasions, had to get her niece or nephew or niece's husband to get me up. I remember the doctors sent us down to some medical department, maybe prosthetics, and they watched me try to move and do certain things. They came forward with a manual wheelchair, transfer board, and a reacher; along with other things that we didn't even know existed. I remember that we were both quite emotional and relieved, that these people truly seemed to care. I remember seeing a look of relief on Deb's face, as we went home with all these new things. Another change was that Deb's nephew, Tom, built a ramp to help me get in the house. Bless his heart. It was a little too steep for me to use with the wheelchair, but it was an immense help. I would crawl up, and Deb would push the wheelchair up the ramp. Then I was given a taste of what's it like to be dependent on a wheelchair, and how people treat you. They don't know how to react. We were at a Golden Corral, that we had gone to a few times. There was a waitress, that seemed to have a distaste for folks in a wheelchair. Deb had put me in the back of the section, so I would be out of the way. She comes up and says "You have to move". I've got a crowd of people coming". She grabs a hold of the wheelchair, and starts to violently shake it. Deb would've liked to knock her out. Her crowd of people never showed up, at least while we were there. Another time at McDonald's, a woman comes up to me where essentially the same thing happened. Time for me to freshen up my coffee, and please be patient with me on this time-line, thing. The awesome parts that we both remember very clearly are coming up. Coming up soon, is when I accepted Christ, our marriage, and my baptism.

7

December 23rd, 2010 at 1:30 am in the morning. I had went into the bedroom, and Deb was asleep. There was some preacher on the TV, but I don't remember who it was. During this time, I wasn't listening to any preachers. He was saying that Jesus was knocking on the door to my heart. It was as if he was talking to just me. He started saying, what I know now to be, the Sinner's Prayer. The church we were attending didn't have altar calls, so I was unaware of what this was. In fact, the knowledge of how to come to Christ, if I had ever been told, had escaped me. I started crying, and felt something that I had never felt before. He was saying this long drawn-out prayer, but because I don't like protocol or long prayers, I just said something like "Okay, I'm yours now Jesus, do whatcha gonna do." I didn't tell Deb. In fact, she didn't know until some months later, that this had happened. I didn't know that I should tell anyone. In my own words, my thinking processes really hadn't changed, and I normally just state that I accepted Christ the best I could at that time.

Are you all following me? Good! There's a lot that I don't remember that Deb does. Do you want her to write this book? That would be absolutely fine with me!! Reminder: I'm writing this book to give those in similar circumstances TRUE HOPE, which is confidant expectation! I've had to write about all the true circumstances of my life up to this time, but hold on we're slowly getting to the amazing, wonderful testimony of

Jesus! No one is ever too far down in life's mess that Jesus can't intervene, whether it's a physical, mental or spiritual mess. Jesus already paid the price, so the answer is there, ready and available.

Let's discuss a wonderful thing that happened. The most lovely woman I've ever known, both inside and outside, agreed that we would get married. This was a very bright spot in during a bad situation. I won't go into all the painful details, but we lost Brandy due to cancer. That is still a very painful memory for both of us, but especially for Deb. The way I proposed was through an internet radio station. The DJ let me propose to her. It was very emotional. The look on Deb's face was precious, as if I were THE most special person on the planet, which I must be, to have her as my wife! Then, we had to decide where to get married. I wanted the pastor from our church to do the ceremony, and Deb agreed. We tried to call him, with no response. A few weeks went by, and we decided to make other plans, since we hadn't been able to reach him. We finally settled on March 12th, 2011. It was to be at Pigeon Forge, TN right by the Smokey Mountains. I had never been there, and it was our first opportunity to actually get away from the trailer. Two weeks from then was to be my first appointment with the new primary care physician at the VA Medical Center, where I had been transferred.

Deb was doing the driving by then instead of me, and she was having to lift the heavy manual wheelchair in and out of the vehicle. Going anywhere was very difficult. In addition, by this time, some of my fingers were curled into the palm, on both hands. I could manipulate them open, and at least have my fingers wrap around the wheel on the wheelchair to get around. We stayed at a pretty nice hotel, where we had gotten a package deal. Deb's nephew, Tom, his wife Kristie, and their daughter, Melanie came. Her other nephew and wife, Justin and Priscilla, along with his brother, Gabe, also attended. It was to be close to a waterfall, which turned out to be very beautiful. The ceremony was beautiful, and we actually have it pretty elaborately on camera. Deb's nephew Tom did a wonderful job snapping pictures, videotaping the ceremony, and Deb looked absolutely gorgeous. The song that played was the Carpenters "White Lace and Promises". It was Deb's choice, and had me tearing up. Deb looked so lovely walking in the grass. The waterfall was the backdrop, and it had just rained so it was loud. No, I absolutely did not wear a suit, but I did wear dress pants, shirt and a tie. We went to Dolly Parton's Rodeo and Ripley's Aquarium. Both places were awesome, but challenging, for someone in a wheelchair. We had to sit on the last row of seats, but it was exciting to watch. Everything we saw at the aquarium was beautiful and it was just awesome to be out of the trailer watching Deb enjoy herself. The sharks and the penguins were a real treat. What gorgeous animals they are. The whole experience was very uplifting and refreshing. This was a very bright spot, in the midst of dark times. I almost forgot, after the ceremony, as we were heading back to the vehicles. The wheelchair started heading towards the river on it's own, I couldn't stop it. Tom caught it, just before me and, it were going to take a plunge, into the water!

8

With that wonderful weekend over, it was time to go to the doctor's appointment and we had no idea what to expect. The primary doctor was a woman, and she was, quite frankly, wonderful. She went over my records, and was convinced that a neurologist was needed. She put in a call for a neurologist to look at me immediately. It was late in the day, but she managed to get the on-call neurologist to come in. We went to the emergency room where he would see us. He told us that he wanted to admit me into the hospital for tests, and this would take a day or two. I ended up being there for three days. It took Deb and her niece to convince me to agree to the admission. Earlier stated was my hatred for doctors. So it took some time for me to be convinced. She ended up sleeping in the car at the hospital garage. She is such an amazing woman. Unknown to me, she spent most of her time praying, which is something she has always done. I just never realized it. Even though I had accepted Jesus, I didn't really have a clue about a prayer life.

Tony, as a hospital patient, was not a pretty picture. I was rude, mean, angry, and absent from the room most of the time. Deb had to go home to take care of our dog Ares and I think, at that time, we had also acquired a stray hound/golden retriever mix, named Ariel. She had wandered into the field, and we took her into to the family. Even though they had put a heart monitor on me, I spent most of my time outside, smoking cigarettes.

The nurse or aide would hunt me down at the smokers station outside. What was supposed to be one day turned into three long days. I seemed to be a very interesting person to visit, because at one time there were five neurologists looking, and prodding at me. This is when they noticed one thing Deb hadn't noticed: my slurring of words. I also had difficulty swallowing, though this hadn't gotten real bad at this time. They did all of their tests, and then talked to Deb and myself. This was when I first heard the words Lou Gehrig's Disease, which until then I had never heard of it. They released me, and during the three hour drive home Deb told me not to go home, and look this disease up. She gave me a short explanation, and stated something about trusting God to heal me. Now remember, up to this point I didn't even own a bible much less know anything about that book! We got home, got settled, and what is the first thing Tony looks up? That is correct, Lou Gehrig's Disease. Deb was in the bedroom walked out; took one look at my face, and said "You read all about it didn't you?" The description seemed to fit, and I think fear and anger hit at the same time. The fighter, inside of me, rose up and was saying "Oh no you don't!", but there was sadness, fear and anger all at the same time.

This seems a good time to mention, that when facing symptoms, do not go on a desperate search for a name or diagnosis. Start speaking against it, which is what Deb did, and I didn't do. There will be more on that subject later. We've got a Baptism to talk about right now, after we get a refreshing cup of black coffee! What is that? You use cream and sugar? THE BLASPHEMY! Just kidding, trying to break the tension. You need some HOPE right now! In Jesus Name Be Healed and have true Hope (confident expectation)!

That weekend, we purchased a bible for me. We went to the church, where we ran into the pastor. This is when I asked him how to go about getting baptized. He said, "First you have to accept Jesus into your heart." I said, "Yup, done deal, did that December 23rd at 1:45 am." Then I showed him the new bible. He then told us to talk to an elder, which just happened to be the same man that had claimed me as his brother in Christ! Up until this point we hadn't gotten to know anyone at the church. As it turned out, we would never see the pastor of the church again, as he was removed from his office. When we would return to the church (for my baptism) the Associate Pastor would baptize me. This was sometime in April, 2011.

Okay, now we've got some bit of background, and something else that we found out, after my healing, to cover first. One Sunday service when there was an increased amount of pain a blond haired lady walked up to me and said, "Are you in a lot of pain? Just hang in there, and keep your focus on Jesus. You will be fine.", or words to that effect. I didn't realize at the time that she was prophesying over me. It turns out, she had a prophetic word (I didn't even know what that was), for me, that I would be healed. She thought it would be at my baptism, which she did attend. She told the Business Manager, at the church, about this prophetic word, and told us after my healing a year plus later. I stated this for a reason. The day, of my Baptism, came around. I'm sure they told me what baptizing was all about, but the reason escaped me at the time. Anyway, the procedure was that an elder had brought a lighter wheelchair, so they could carry me up the many steps into the baptismal. First, I had to transfer into that chair, then four men would carry me up the steps, and then we'd go through the ceremony. That went according to plan. Then they got me up the steps into the water........then they let go. The chair, and me, went backwards into the water! It was hilarious! They caught me, just before my face entered the water. Then the elder of the church spoke some words, as he spoke I felt tingling all over my body especially my legs. The thought crossed my mind, "Stand up and walk". The second thought was "Idiot you can't walk", so I didn't even try to get up. This was one of three different occasions that this happened. I want to say this. We have to have HOPE, which is Confident Expectation! I didn't try to move, because I had no expectation of being healed. Instead, I grabbed the negative thought thrown into my mind by the enemy. Quick lesson there! Then I was dunked into the water, and pulled back-up. I was in tears. It was very emotional for me. Before they carried the wheelchair down the steps. I got changed, and transferred back to my wheelchair. Then went back out to the sanctuary. Another weird thing was; they were singing a song, and I felt some sensation sweep over me. As I was singing, my wife looks at me and whispers, "You were singing in tongues!" I think I actually just dismissed that, thinking that Deb had just not been hearing me correctly, or it was just me slurring my words. It was at my Baptism that the Holy Spirit told Deb that I would live and not die.

9

At another doctor visit to see the neurologist, the Chief of Neurology, explained that he was, in-fact, leaning towards Lou Gehrig's and that we should think about moving closer to the hospital. We did indeed entertain that idea for a bit. We even spent one day looking at houses, but then decided against it. The neurologist set-up an appointment for me to see a urologist, which would happen after the next huge event. My parents, my sister Angela, my brother Mark and his wife Rachel came for a visit.

This was in July 2011, and in my mind, it was their farewell visit with me. I had never met Rachel, and had not seen Angela as an adult. It had been over twenty years since I had seen any of them. Over the years, we had kept in touch somewhat, but our relationship had always been strained, mostly due to my actions and behavior. This was the first time that they met Deb and she, of course, met their criteria with flying colors. It was a short two-day visit, if memory serves me correctly.

The most memorable thing, I will never forget is "The Pinnacle." In Middlesboro, KY there is a spot that leads up the Cumberland Mountains. There's a spot, that has been marked on the ground. It is where VA, KY and TN all meet. There are stairs, but as you can imagine, it is very steep and long. My parents were interested in going up, and a split second decision was made, that my brother and father would carry me up it in the wheelchair. They were serious, but my reaction was. "You all go, I'll just stay down here." My father has just turned eighty, so that would've made him seventy-four at the time. A manual wheelchair weighs at least fifty pounds by itself, add to that my one hundred and twenty some pounds, going essentially straight-up. Think of this, at my baptism it took four men to go up only about fourteen steps, with a lighter wheelchair, which was a truly amazing feat! Overall, it was a very fun time, and nice to re-connect with my family. Another event, on that visit, was going to eat at a fancy resort. Whatever I ordered, I could only eat a few bites. My slurred speech really started to get worse while there, and trying to talk was very embarrassing. My speech would come and go. Sometimes it would be understandable, but other times it would sound like gibberish. At that dinner, I was not understandable. I hated it, and was very embarrassed. Everyone loved Deb. They told her how glad they were, that she was my wife. My brother made a comment about how surprised he was that I hadn't cussed one time.

The next day, we met at the hotel to say goodbye. They were on their way home, and we were on our way to the doctor. On this visit, we visited the primary care doctor, and she was appalled at how quickly I had gone downhill. She reviewed my records, and gave me a provi-sional diagnosis of ALS/ Lou Gehrig's Disease. She wanted to start the process of getting all the help we would need to make life bearable. I blurted out of nowhere, "Jesus is going to heal me" and I surprised my-self that I said it. She sent in a nurse and a social worker, and I told them the same thing! Quick lesson, a declaration stated without HOPE (con-fident expectation) means nothing. It can be bold, but without expec-tation behind it, nothing will manifest. Another lesson is that, when a declaration is made with the thought that you will be healed, because of your words, nothing will happen. These were some lessons learned after my healing. At the time, I truly thought I was believing those words, but nothing happened. My wife, on the other hand, acted with true bold-ness and expectation. The social worker told her that she needed to join an ALS support group, and apply for me to be put in a nursing home for veterans. Deb, replied, "I accept that he is sick, and that's all I'm going to do, and will care for him". In my record, the social worker recorded that she felt Deb was in denial. We found out about this, when we were in front of the judge for my Social Security disability. Deb wasn't in denial, but in acceptance of the Truth!

10

Another thing the doctor did was send me to Prosthetics to get fitted for a motorized wheelchair. They looked at me, pulling and tugging on my arms and legs, looking at my movement etc. Remarking that they had to be sure that they ordered the right chair, to suit all my needs, present and future. A Quantum Four chair was decided upon, and they also ordered a ramp to be installed on our trailer, so I could more easily get in and out. This is actually an important point, because unknown to us the next few months would be warfare with the VA. The facility, that to this point had been supportive and doing their best to meet my medical needs, would start to go in the opposite direction. Up to this time, I still had to either crawl up the ramp that Tom had made or sit on the steps and scoot up them, which was becoming more and more difficult. One thing I will say is, unknown to us, there had just been a law passed that ALS was automatically service-connected, and maybe this is why, the upcoming circumstances happened. I don't know. It is irrelevant to us now, but at the time it was crazy nonsense that made my life almost unbearable. We'll get to those issues, but I digress. At the time, we were told that, in a few days, someone would come out to the house, and decide how to build a wheelchair ramp. We were also told that the wheelchair should arrive in a few weeks, and that our vehicle would be equipped to carry the wheelchair.

Okay, break time for me! This next part has some anger attached with it, in regard, to how I was treated. I have forgiven the people involved, but just telling this part of the story is stirring up some emotion. Please bear with me, and here is the thing. If things had happened any differently, my healing may not have happened. Most importantly, I do not want this part to overshadow how GOOD God is, and how awesome that Jesus willingly gave Himself so that my healing could happen!!! Along with my healing, comes an awesome testimony for you to be encouraged by!!

My wife and I waited to hear information on the ramp and the wheelchair, but after three weeks there was no news. An appointment with the chief neurologist was coming, and we decided that we would check then. Both things had become of the up-most importance, as my physical body continued to deteriorate. The manual wheelchair was becoming more difficult for me to manipulate, and going out of the trailer was a very time and energy consuming chore. Imagine this, the doors of the trailer sit about eight to ten feet above the ground. The door on the other side is about four feet from the ground, making for a very tough time when primarily using only your arms! Invariably, I didn't leave the trailer much during this time. It was also getting harder and harder for me to get into the vehicle. My wife had to endure lifting the very heavy wheelchair, which had her back all torn up. It created her own set of health problems to deal with, which she did without complaining. Knowing how this was affecting her, really tore me up inside. I hated that she had to put herself through all of that. More on this issue later.

We went to the appointments with the neurologist, and the other with the urologist. The appointment with the neurologist was bad. He looked at me, and stated that there was nothing neurologically wrong with me. This was a huge blow, and hit us both like a ton of bricks!! Honestly, he was fortunate that I wasn't able to do anything, or he would have been beaten to a pulp! Fighting was still my first reaction to things. My body just wasn't able to carry out what I wanted to do. Here is where an interjection is needed. Those, facing a similar circumstance, embrace a non-diagnosis. If a doctor tells you they can't find anything wrong, don't go out on a mission to prove them wrong. The enemy wants us to do that.

He wants us to solidify and declare, that we are sick. Instead, we should rejoice, and thank The Father and Jesus that nothing was found. We should cling with an expectation that all the symptoms will leave and that we will return back to health. Had I done that then, there is the real possibility that the next year of suffering wouldn't have happened. Focus on the finished work of Jesus, first. He paid for you to be healthy. We left his office, and went to the urologist appointment. Deb stayed in the waiting room. The urologist said to my face that there was no test that could be conducted (we later found out that was a lie), that my symptoms were neurological, and I would just have to deal with it. This was about me being unable to urinate, but feeling full all the time and my bowels were inactive as well. In my medical records, he wrote "The patient drinks too many fluids, possibly neurological, but I doubt it. "Are you for real!!!??? I was barely drinking two cups a day, which was mainly coffee. The two doctors had totally contradicted, each other! This particular part, we found out about several weeks later. At the time, I told my wife what he had told me. It was neurological, and there was nothing that could be done. It was a double blow, that we had been dealt.

Next, we went to Prosthetics, to find out that neither the wheelchair, nor the ramp, had even been ordered. It was as if the ground, and I do mean the ground, had been pulled right out from under us. We headed to the Director of the VA's Office. I do not even remember that conversation. I do know that I was struggling with even talking at all, let alone coherently. The whole conversation must have ended well, because within a few days a man arrived at the door. He was there to assess how to build the ramp. We never heard back from him. A few more days went by, and I called him. He said that the VA hadn't approved his plans. We called the Director again, and then finally a ramp was set up. Roughly a month later, a woman showed up with the wheelchair. She instructed us how to use it. I was so excited, because I would be able to get out of the trailer more often!!

Grab a cup of coffee, and hold your breath; the woes, with the ramp, were not quite over yet. When the ramp was set-up, there had been a deck with stairs. The people, putting the ramp in, ripped the stairs off, and left the deck. When I would go out the door, the deck would be what the wheelchair would run over first. Remember also, this was about ten feet from the ground. One evening, as I was exiting the trailer, the deck collapsed; and myself, sitting in the wheelchair, fell to the ground. Deb called the rescue team. I was unhurt, but they had to figure out how to get the three-hundred and fifty plus pound wheelchair into the trailer, so it could be used by me. It was amazing, that the wheelchair itself, was unscathed. They somehow managed to get the wheelchair into the trailer. The deck had been about five feet long. Imagine lifting that thing over the gap into the trailer! The amazing thing is, one of those on the rescue team, met me again, and saw my condition roughly three years later. They would meet me this time: healed, healthy, and hear my testimony of how Jesus had healed me. Thank You Jesus!

The next day we called the ramp people. They came out, and looked at the situation. They decided what it would take to fix it, and turned in the request to the VA. They denied the request to fix it. Meanwhile, I was stuck in the trailer with no exit! The other door was too narrow for the wheelchair, without tearing the door frame apart. We had to deal with the "Demonic VA" as I was now referring to them. It was roughly a week, and lot's of phone calls to the VA, before they would finally approve the repairs and get it fixed. We did have to pay for the debris of broken wood to be cleared away.

The other thing is this. We had no way to transport myself and the wheelchair. Even though, by law, the VA had provided me with the wheelchair. They were supposed to provide a means of transporting the wheelchair. Their reasoning was that the vehicle we owned would not support the weight of the wheelchair, and they requested that we buy another vehicle. Here is the thing, when we bought the Equinox, they told us it would support any type of wheelchair. We had no way of transporting the wheelchair, and this greatly reduced my being able to travel. In the year 2012, when my condition further worsened, we would have to struggle getting me transferred from the motorized wheelchair to the manual one to the vehicle. Then my wife would have to lift the manual wheelchair into the vehicle.

There were other things going on at this time. This is all around October 2011. My Social Security disability had been approved, so I was now on Medicare. We decided to give up on the VA, and to stop looking to them for help. An appointment was scheduled with a civilian doctor. In order to do that, we had to arrange for the medical records to be transferred to the doctor. This is when we discovered what the urologist and neurologist, at the VA had written. We later decided to contact our congressman. We told them all that had transpired, and they opened an investigation. This investigation actually occurred later, after I had seen the civilian neurologist and urologist. They both proved that what I was going through, was in fact without a doubt, a neurological disease. The result of the investigation? The congressman informed my wife and I, that all of the stuff from the VA, was simply a "typo". Nothing was ever done about it. Because of that my wife and I suffered through all of this without help. My wife would search the internet for hours looking for an organization that might help us. One was never found. I am jumping ahead of the story a bit, so bear with me!

11

We will return back to the continuing saga of the medical side of things, and how helpful the civilian doctors were later. Let's talk about the practical daily life. Deb, at the time of my Baptism, received a comforting word from The Holy Spirit, "He shall live and not die and declare the works of The Lord." In her own words, after the healing, she told me that all she knew is that the disease wouldn't take my life. It never occurred to her, that I would be healed. Every time I would speak death, she would speak this scripture. I would state that I was going to die. She would say that I would live and not die and declare the Word of the Lord. When she wasn't taking care of my needs, she would be praying. She is a truly an outstanding woman of God! She would spend her days praying, and also searching the Internet for an organization that would help us.

Our trailer is 64 feet long and a single wide, so at this point my motorized wheelchair put several holes in the hallway walls. It was a very tight fit through the doorway to the bedroom, and there wasn't room to move it out of the way. It would block the doorway. Also, I couldn't transfer myself from the wheelchair to the bed any longer. The living room ended up being, where I would spend my days and nights. I was preoccupied, with searching the internet, for information about Lou Gehrig's; and spent my days on-line with an ALS Support Group. This, honestly, did nothing more than put my mental state in further depression. After my healing,

I would revisit this group, tell them my testimony; and be put out of it, blocked for life. At night I would transfer myself to the couch. There did come a time when that would stop, and I would stay in the wheelchair. A bright spot would be Ariel, the stray hound/lab/retriever, she had puppies. She had five puppies. We kept one of them, who we called Angel. When Angel was born, Ariel didn't rip the sack open for her to breathe. I ended up doing that for her; saving her life. Angel would sleep beside me on the couch, and she was a great comfort. At this time, we had Ares, Ariel, Angel and a barn cat that we called Kitty. One day the cat had walked in the house went up to big ole Ares, stuck it's butt in his face and just stayed here ever since. That cat would spend hours in my lap. I was stuck in the living room 24 hours a day. We do have a bathroom there; but its there in the hallway, past the kitchen. It also fell victim to the wheelchair. I would navigate the wheelchair to the start of the hallway, fall out of it, and then crawl/pull myself to the bathroom. You get the picture. My knees pretty much stayed a bloody mess even with pads on them.

We had very few visitors, or anyone that would come and help out. We were both in isolation. Once every few weeks, a woman from the church, would call to ask how we were. We appreciated that very much. At one point, a fellow who was a carpenter, came at our request to give an estimate on how to open up the bathroom. This would make the wheelchair fit through the door, and make it easier on me. It would've cost around five grand, that we didn't have. The lady from church, Yvonne, did do an awesome thing. She would send the church van out to our place on Sundays, which was actually a good distance from the church. They would then get me in the van, and load my manual wheelchair. There came a time though when I just couldn't physically handle it. One such time, she came with her teenage son. They were in her truck, and they literally had to drag me into the vehicle. I won't forget that time. There was an occasion when a man, who would later become that church's pastor, was driving the van and he mentioned to me Paul's thorn in the flesh. I believe that was the first time I had heard of it. He explained to me that this referred to a disease, and that Paul stopped praying after three times for it to be taken away. God said NO! In all fairness to this man, I don't know whether that is what he said, or if that was my perception. I only let the elders, of the church, pray their begging prayers three times over me. My Friends, Please Understand This, it is God's Will that all be healed, cause Jesus already paid for it. When it comes to sickness the answer is never no. I'll explain it in further detail in my next book. Paul was not referring to a disease, but to persecution by men towards Paul. Please do not use this as I did. It is a false comfort keeping you sick! This was the second thing, that I studied in depth after my healing. It is one of my all time pet peeves, because as was stated, I used it. Another van driver, Edward, was so awesome; and such an encouragement. He truly is an awesome Man of God with a servant's heart.

Okay, so that brings us up to date till around December 2011. You get the picture. Life was not easy at all. Day in and day out, Deb had to manage everything on her own, including dealing with an angry, stubborn and depressed invalid!

12

Deb, never wavered in her faith! There is Our Heavenly Father first, Jesus and then Deb. Everyday, for three years, she was praying and declaring my healing in the bedroom. She stayed strong, even when everything around us caved in. She did not let my continuing downward spiral sway her faith. As my utterings turned more and more to death, she was declaring life. I had gone from that person, who had boldly declared Jesus would heal him, to one that had lost all hope. There was a day when I fell out of the wheelchair, and refused to let her get someone to me back into the wheelchair. I struggled on the floor for almost three hours and saw her peeping around the corner crying. I did manage to make it back into the wheelchair. I still believe that angels lifted me, back into it.

Another time, two of our dogs, Ares and Ariel, escaped from their yard. They were gone for around a week. We thought we had lost them. All I saw was hopelessness; all she saw was Jesus. Please take this to heart. Whether a care-giver or the sick person, do not take my example. Take Deb's example. The phrase "Don't get your hopes up" is a deadly phrase. Instead get your HOPE (your confident expectation) sky high. The higher your expectations are; the closer to your miracle you are.

Around this time, we went to the civilian doctor. On the first visit, he had such compassion, and a true desire to help. He made an appointment for me to see a very good neurologist, and got paperwork going for me to receive a Home Health Care team. Folks, the shining light is just around the corner. Unknown to me, things would change dramatically for the better in a way that I could never have dreamed. First, we're going to take a mop to a few things, and cover the civilian neurologist's visit. We saw the civilian neurologist a total of three times. The initial consultation visit, he had all my records from the VA which were paper copies, it was many pages. He tugged, pulled, and found out how utterly invalid I was. He asked what would help to make me the most comfortable. We told him about my bladder, and the fact that I couldn't relieve myself easily. It was really not much at all. He ordered an EMG, and sent me to a urologist. The female doctor came in, and talked to us for about five minutes. Then said she was going to do a test. This is when I found out that the VA urologist had lied to me about not having a test to discover the true problem. I think the test is called a Fill test, but I'm not sure. Anyway, she did the test, and discovered that it was in fact neurological. It's called a neurogenic bladder. This also totally confirms the lie, that was spoken by the VA Chief of Neurology. When he said that nothing neurological was wrong with me. I received a little bit of vindication there. This does confirm, what was upcoming, has to be recognized as a true miracle. The kicker is this. In order to get me some relief, all this doctor had to do was increase a medication, that I was already taking. It did not give me full relief, but it sure did help a whole lot!

The second trip to the neurologist, he stated that my condition was like nothing he had ever seen before. He told us that it was a completely unknown neurological disorder. There was absolutely no hope for survival, because my central nervous system was completely shutting down. (I don't remember his exact words, but that is the way I remember it). Medically, there was nothing he could do. It was then that I was so ready to just give up and die. I wouldn't tell my wife that, but turns out she knew that I had given up! INTERJECTION: Never give up! The enemy can't win, if you don't give up. I do not care how hopeless it may appear. Learn from my story, and do not give up! The only power the enemy has is deceit and lies. Yes, he can and will use the most compassionate people to get us to accept those lies! I SPEAK LIFE INTO YOUR BODY, BE HEALED AND DO NOT GIVE UP!

The Lord is wonderful though. He was about to place three people into our lives, that would shed some light into our very dark landscape. Around this time period, I ate the last solid food, that I would have until after my healing. We went to the Cracker Barrel, where we ordered my favorite food: Country Fried Steak. I couldn't swallow, so it just hung there in my throat, and I couldn't breathe at all. I do not know how, but somehow it got dislodged. That was the last solid food that I even attempted to eat. I think that was about six months out from my healing, Deb thinks it was somewhere between three to four months out. We're both terrible with dates and time, so take your pick. Did I mention that every year we forget our anniversary, seriously! My brother always sends us a card the day after our anniversary. Then I go to my wife, and pretend like I remembered it, and that she alone, forgot it. Nope never works!

Home Health Caregivers are precious to both myself and to Deb. If you are a Home Health Care Provider, please know that we thank you for what you do! Words will never express correctly, what you mean to those you provide service for. My team consisted of a nurse, a physical therapist, and a speech/swallowing therapist. They are kind, compassionate, and precious even with a somewhat difficult patient. We won't mention my name there. My team gave me contact with other people, and credit is given to them for stirring up an amount of hope in me. Each helped, in their own way. The nurse was kind and compassionate. The physical therapist forced me to push myself, and was caring. The speech swallowing therapist kept my mind alert and active. When they walked through that door, it was as if a light was turned on. They each played a part in sustaining me long enough for me to receive my healing.

Here I need to mention the doctor that had gotten me the Home-Health Care team, and sent me to the neurologist and urologist. He had to have been sent by God. He had just moved here, and was in our area long enough to get me set-up with those wonderful folks. Then he moved back to where he came from. I've never even been able to thank him. Dr. Wiesnoff, is what I believe his name was. THANK YOU! Because he moved, we had to find another doctor, and had to visit his office. He was a believer, who had been recommended by the Home-Health Care nurse. She had to have a doctor to send her reports to. On these trips, I always managed somehow to help Deb out by squirming or wiggling, but in some way managing to help her. After we saw the doctor, and she was getting me into the car. My whole body just froze solid and stiff like a board. She had to get help with me, and these are just a few of the struggles we went through.

13

We are here folks. Thank you for reading. The stage has been set, and enough background information given. What say you? Are you ready for a miracle? Hold that thought! I need ....you guessed it, some more coffee! We are now at May 2012, and two months before my healing. My physical condition at this point, according to my memory, was: a severe "all-the-time" headache, eyebrows were paralyzed, extra saliva, difficulty swallowing, severe emphysema, sleep apnea, slurring words, high blood pressure, fingers contorted into a fist, arms weak, can move forearms maybe eight inches, could not raise arms, gastroparesis (stomach paralysis), neurogenic bladder, bowels not moving, legs useless, many back problems including disc-deterioration disorder, bulging discs, and herniated discs. There's probably more, but I do believe that you get the picture! My body is a mere shell.

Around May, Deb took the Equinox to get it detailed, in order to trade it in for a wheelchair van. Then I could travel, and get out of that trailer. On the way home, she felt her peace about the trade-in diminishing, a sickening feeling, as if she shouldn't do it. The 2010 Chevrolet Equinox, with 50,000 miles, was going to be traded in for a wheelchair van a 2007, with some 200,000 miles. She came home, and said she felt Holy Spirit guiding her to not do the trade-in. Around that same time, a contractor came to the house, because we had been considering having a disabled home built.

He was coming to see what our requirements were in order for him to draw up plans, and give us an estimate. We never saw him again!

In June, we attended church, the latest preacher gave a sermon in which he stated, pointing at me, that if you're not healed it's because you don't have enough faith. I was furious, after-all I was the one that had told the doctors, that Jesus would heal me. I do know what it feels like to have someone say those particular words to you, in this type of setting. Quick sermon: We all have the measure of faith. We believers have the spirit of faith, The Holy Spirit. That faith simply needs to be empowered with the correct beliefs, which activates our Hope (confidant Expectation), which then empowers our faith to be seen. Got it, get it . . ..good!

Although at that time, I would have told you that I had no faith. This was before I had studied the scriptures. At that point, my days were spent trying to figure out how to kill myself. Two weeks prior to my healing, I tried to run my wheelchair into the four lane highway, that was by the trailer. I spent forty-five minutes, while Deb was out shopping, trying to get someone/anyone to hit me. Obviously, no one did, and that stupid wheelchair was too slow. Deb later told me that whenever she would leave the trailer. The thought would come to her, that when she came back home she would find me dead. So, she knew my thoughts all along! Once she left the trailer, that thought would leave, and she would be comforted, knowing that I would live.

One week before my healing, the speech and swallowing therapist walked into the trailer white as a ghost. He said that he had seen me walking up the road. In other words, he had seen a vision of me walking. I thought, "Idiot, I've been here all day!" The next day, the physical therapist left our house almost in tears, because of how much my body had deteriorated. Understand that the Home-Health Care and Physical Therapy programs must show that they are working, and if the person isn't making improvement. Hospice is, then, the next step, which is "waiting for the person to die." I was right at that point the therapist thought, and being such a caring person, didn't want to see this happen. I believe that he knew if he put me on hospice, it would be lights-out, the end, throw my body in a cave!

One week later, on July fourth 2012, I woke up, and was still embracing death. I just wanted it to be finished, and over with. I was tired of suffering, and tired of seeing Deb put through all of the stress and heartache. In my mind, I went over and over a check list of ways to kill myself, but couldn't think of a way, that I was physically able to do. I found a web-site that was about healing, and it had a technique on the site, by a Christian man. I looked it over, and this sparked something in me, I do believe. I mention this in my later church testimony. Later, after my healing, I did research on that, and I was thankful that I didn't /couldn't do the positions it showed on there, as they are demonic positions. Please be careful, there are things out there that claim to be Christian that aren't. Instead, they are thinly disguised, and cannot be supported by scripture. I Thank God, that didn't happen. I mention it because I have been asked about it, and thought it was important to add. There was, however a part on the website about love, and saying you love yourself. I do believe that seeing the word Love did come to my mind. It is all about His Love for us on the Cross! It was a few hours later, that I started thinking about Jesus, and how much He had suffered for me! My thought was that Jesus had suffered far more than I was suffering. I started imagining Jesus at the whipping post. I looked at the clock, and it was 1:45 PM. At some point this became an open vision, and I was in front of Jesus, as He was receiving the thirty-nine lashes. I saw chunks of his flesh being torn from his body. The whip curling around his back to his chest tearing chunks of skin from His front side as well as from His back. What I saw was more horrific than anything I had thought of before. Than the image changed to the cross, and I was standing right below Him. I looked up, saw His ribs and when I looked into His eyes, I saw Love. Above Him, I saw a black funnel cloud pour into him. The image was like billions of flies in a funnel formation. Around Him, I saw dark shadows laughing, waiting to devour Him (after my healing I read Psalm 22, and this all made sense). Jesus loves me! I saw His Eyes again. The pain the agony was all there, but mostly what I saw was LOVE. Jesus Loves Me! Jesus' body did not even resemble a man's body. It was unrecognizable, but His eyes. I was the reason that He was on that cross, because He Loves Me. I felt a peace that I had never known, and out loud I said, "Jesus Loves Me, Jesus Loves Me, Jesus Loves Me." Then I said, "Back Pain Leave, Back Pain Leave, Back Pain Leave"; and then "In Jesus Name", "In Jesus Name", "In Jesus Name". Then, I suddenly recognized the back pain was completely gone! I did a double- take. The back pain, that had been so severe for over four years, had suddenly left. Then I thought to myself, Oh My Gosh! Then I said "fingers move" "fingers move" "fingers move" Thank You Jesus! They uncurled, and I could move them! My wheelchair had been in the corner, of the living room. If you could see me right now, I'm pointing to where it was. I went down the hallway to the bedroom. Deb's jaw dropped; a look of shock came over her face. I'm not sure if, at that point, her brain was actually registering what was happening! "Jesus willing, I'll be back walking" is what I stated, and went back out to the living room. I said "Jesus don't let me fall, legs move". It was as if they both moved at the same time. They hit the floor, and once again I said "Thank You Jesus, don't let me fall". I stood up and started walking. Deb said that I looked like Frankenstein, but I was walking! My voice cleared up, I was able to lift my arms above my head! Thank You Jesus! Deb went to get her niece and her son, Gabe. She had me hide in the bedroom, then said "Come out". When I walked out, they seemed in shock as well. Actually, I do believe we were all in shock and amazement! I remember going to let the dogs in, and it seemed that the door had shrunk. Seriously, the doorway seemed so small all of the sudden. When I went to grab the doorknob, it wasn't there! Everything was as if it were brand-new, and I was doing it for the first time. I made a short video, which I sent to my Mother, Father, and Mark showing me standing, walking, and bending over. They replied that I seemed "Awfully somber!" Somber I may have been, but I was thanking Jesus every other word.

Deb remembered that our church, with another church, was having a worship service for the Fourth of July holiday. We didn't even know what time it started. We called Joe, the worship service leader, and asked him what time it started. We told him that we had something to show him. We discussed it, and decided to go ahead and leave. We were so excited, and wanted to share that moment with everyone. We would be an hour or two early, but who cared! We did decide to take the manual wheelchair, because the service was outside. We had no idea about the sitting arrangement. I actually helped Deb load it up. Remember this point. Then we were standing beside the vehicle, and Deb said, "Go get in the passenger side." "No", I said "I'm driving". She said, "No you aren't. It's been three years since you've driven." I was stubborn, she lifted her hands up and said, "Okay, I don't care if we get in a wreck, you're healed! Thank You Jesus." With that settled, we took off with me driving.

We arrived at the parking lot of Goody's, where the service was being held. Lo and behold the first person we saw was Yvonne, the church business manager. I got out of the vehicle, we went to the back, and took the wheelchair out. I started walking towards Yvonne, and she got excited, started texting, and calling people. Then she shot the video of me walking, and then bending and touching the ground. After that video was shot, I told Deb I was fine, and wouldn't need the wheelchair. I went to put it back into the vehicle. I lifted it myself! That is how dramatically my strength was returning. It was hot, so Deb asked if I wanted some water, and that she could use some. I told her that I would get it, walked to the tent got the water, and opened the cap by myself. Small task for some, but to me it was huge! At this point, Yvonne asked if I was hungry, and at that time I felt a burning in my stomach. At first I was questioning what was going on, but Deb said "You're hungry!" It had been so long, since I had been hungry, I wasn't even recognizing that's what it was. Yvonne said she and her husband would like to take us to Cracker Barrel, and we said "Sure". Because we were early, there was time. It was right across from where we were. We jumped in Rick's vehicle and went. When we got there, Rick, watching me walk, stated that with each step, I was getting steadier and stronger. In front of the door of Cracker Barrel was a man in a wheelchair. I walked up to him and I told him, "I was just healed by Jesus, In Jesus Name Be Healed, Get up and Walk". I made one error. As I looked down I saw he had no legs. Honestly, that killed my expectation. This was my first time praying for the sick. We talked for a minute, and all was good. I gave him a short version of my testimony, and he started to cry with joy for me. Inside we went, and would you like to guess, what I ate? I ordered what my last meal had been many months before: Country Fried Steak. Yvonne actually has my first bite on video. I cleaned the plate off eating everything! When we returned for the worship service, everyone came running up to me. While we had been eating, many people had been texting, and making phone calls to people; telling them that I had been healed. People were coming out of the woodwork! Edward, the van driver, was there, and said someone had called him, and that he hadn't planned on coming, until they had told him that I was healed. Also, Tom (Deb's Nephew), who she had called, was driving on patrol in that parking lot. Deb ran up to the vehicle and said "Look at how good he's walking! Then Joe came up, and said that they wanted me to give my testimony to everyone. When they called me forward out of the crowd, I actually felt like jumping onto the stage, but when I got there it was a lot higher than it looked. I opted out, heading for the stairs instead. By this time there was probably a thousand people there. Wow! I gave my testimony, and the biggest thing I stated was "The Lord Healed Me. He wants you healed. He paid for every person to be saved and healed. He wants every person healed." Oh my gosh, after my testimony, I don't know how many people I talked to, or prayed for that night. One thing I do remember is one man coming up to me, and said you're wrong, as he threw some scriptures at me. I had no response, I didn't know the scriptures, yet! I almost forgot, one song that the band kept playing was God is Love by Jonathon David Helser. I had heard it before, but now it had special meaning. "Walk on the waves of the storm" I played it continually for months afterwords; singing it even while walking the dogs.

Ok, time for a break, we still have some more ground to be covered, but in the mean-time; Be Healed In Jesus Name.

When we got home that night I tried to listen to my favorite Ozzy Osbourne album and couldn't. I got physically ill. I tried to watch a horror movie and couldn't I got physically ill. I had changed so quickly, that my wife was amazed at the changes in me. The next day I started reading, and studying the Bible. Remember that Bible, that I had bought before my Baptism? It finally got used! Also, my healing was on a Wednesday. By Saturday, I was on the side of the hill at the church using my weed eater! I started walking our dogs Ariel, Ares and Angel about four miles a day!

I digress. The next day the home-health care nurse came. I saw her car coming up the gravel driveway. The wheelchair was there. When the door was opened. She could see it. I stepped out from behind the door! Her reaction was precious. She sat down, and I told her what had transpired. We told her about how I ate at the Cracker Barrel, she said, "There is no doubt that Jesus healed you. Your body should have gone into shock after going so long with no solid food." She said, "You still took your medication, right?" My wife and I looked at each other. We had completely forgotten about the eighteen some medications that I had been on. She said, "Okay, let me check you out." She took my blood pressure, and it was absolutely normal. She listened to my stomach, and although she had never heard my stomach move before, "She said that now it was growling like a lion"! It was perfect! She checked my reflexes; saw me walk, and was amazed. We were all excitedly praising The Lord. She stated that she would keep checking up on me for few more weeks, before releasing me. I asked her not to tell Mr. Lee the physical therapist! I had something very special in mind for him!

I saw his vehicle pulling in. He got out, and went to the trunk of his car, as I'd seen him do a million times before. I snuck up behind him, and hollered," Mr. Lee you are so fired"!! He jumped, looked at me, and said, "Tony what did you do?" I said, "Not a thing, Jesus did it!" He was so excited praising the Lord. He stated that he'd seen some wonderful miracles before, but nothing like this. We talked for a while, and I gave him the full run down. He said, that he would continue to check in on me for a few weeks, and make sure all was going well.

Now for the speech and swallowing therapist; when he came up, I met him at his vehicle and said, "This time you're seeing me walk for real!!" He came inside, and I told him what had happened. He was speechless, and kept looking at my tattoo. Oops, I forgot to tell you after the original diagnosis, I had gotten a tattoo that had the letters TIG on my forearm upside down, the meaning was: Trust In God. After my healing, I went, and had a sun, and dove added to it. He kept looking at it, and said it was shining brightly on my forearm. It was obvious that something was going on there! Another tattoo, that I had added is on my left bicep. I have a wheelchair with a red circle around it, and a red slash through it; signifying no wheelchair. On my right bicep, is a tattoo that had my former long forgotten street name Gypsy Man on it. That one now has a cross. Gypsy Man is forever crucified, and put to death by the cross. Amen to that!!

As for the regular doctors, one by one I made appointments, and went to all of them, except for the Chief of Neurology at the VA and that urologist at the VA. I did go back to the VA primary care physician, the civilian neurologist, the civilian urologist, and all were amazed. They all confirmed what I already knew, that I was indeed healed.

14

Immediately after my healing I started to study the scriptures for myself. For a year and a half, I had no influences other than scripture, and Holy Spirit. I was a clean slate, spending up to twelve hours a day studying. Seeking to know only Truth, we continued to go to the church we were attending, when I was healed. After a year, we left, as I was studying and learning on my own, I started hearing things in that church, that didn't meet up with scripture. I will leave that at that. I got a job driving people to their medical appointments. Then a year ago, I started my own company getting odors out of used cars. These are/were both wonderful opportunities to pray for healing, see people saved, and to share my testimony. Through this all, one thing that I started doing right from my healing, that continues to this day, is: praying for the sick, and seeing them healed. Roughly, it took about a week of me praying for people to start getting results. This is something I want to stress. Every single believer can, and should pray for the sick, and see results. It is my desire to preach the full Gospel with signs, wonders and miracles accompanying. I have done this for four years now. I am so thankful with the way things worked out, because my foundational teachings of the scriptures had been done with the Holy Spirit, before I heard other teachings. There are preachers, that simply confirmed what I had learned on my own through Holy Spirit, experiences, and studying scripture. I have given my testimony on Healing Miracles TV with Joan Able, and on Heal the Sick Podcast with Millian Quinteros. I am a host trainer, at a free online school called Inside Out Healing and Equipping School, although currently I'm on a hiatus. As far as those that teach healing, currently, I agree most with Curry Blake of John G. Lake Ministries. I do recommend that you check out the free school that Cheryl Fritz founded : Inside Out Training and Equipping School (**www.insideouttrainingandequippingschool.org**) on Facebook. This school does a good job at giving the basics of healing; and opportunity to get firsthand experience at healing the sick, in a safe environment. They offer many other free classes as well, check them out.

There are two things that have continued to happen. Every person I meet gets a very short testimony of my healing, and they also get prayed for; specifically they get their physical condition spoken to with the authority of Christ. Since my healing, I have seen many wonderful healings. The Truth is, that the same sacrifice Jesus paid for our Salvation, He also paid for our healing. The Truth is that every Believer can pray for the sick, and see them healed. There should not be a separate healing ministry. Just as every believer is responsible for sharing the Gospel to unbelievers, every believer can, and should be praying for the sick and seeing them healed. It started for me with my healing, but didn't stop there. As I live my daily life, I minister to those I meet. During that first week of my healing, while we were ordering Wendy's, I told the woman taking our order about my miracle. My wife and I constantly stop, and give witness to people about my healing. Then we declare/pray for their healing. Healing isn't a mystery anymore than salvation is. My goal is to minister salvation and healing to all those I meet; and to teach others to do the same thing. Jesus paid the price when He hung on the cross. He became sin, so that Tony Myers, a former atheist, could be saved, healed, set free, and made whole. Jesus died to give Tony a choice: He did the same for you, "Choose this day Life or Death; choose Life!"

The only reason we have to teach, about healing, is because of the many wrong beliefs, that have come from man and not from God. My healing destroys many of the teachings, that are being taught in churches. These mis-teachings do not come from The Father, or Son, or from the scriptures. I am currently planning on writing two additional books. One on the subject of healing, where I will deliver an in-depth teaching on what I've been shown; and another one once you are healed, how to keep your healing.

15

For the first year after my healing, it was a true learning experience. There was no one around me, that had an experience like mine. My life had been over. I was at the end of it, and then suddenly to have a chance at a future again! I am always truly grateful to the Father and Jesus, for my healing, but I also had many lessons to be learned. Struggles to go through, which I wish to share! I was like a newborn babe, but with the mind of an adult. Below are some of the many testimonies I have of, some of the healings that I've been a part of.

A woman in her fifties, who had a severed nerve in her hand, and also had a broken neck. She couldn't turn her head, and she had a pacemaker. I prayed for her hand first, and her fingers started to move. We declared a bit more over it, and then her strength returned to her fingers. She was able to use it normally. Then we commanded her neck to be healed, and she was able to move her head as any normal person could. Then I had her command her heart to be healed, and the pacemaker (which she could feel), disappear. She felt a burning sensation, and then she couldn't find the pacemaker anymore.

A man had a back that been broken, and surgical rods were implanted, along with a hip replacement. I prayed first for his hip, which had been replaced. He felt a burning, then felt a hip bone had replaced the steel hip bone replacement. It was very emotional. He accepted Christ, and then I told him to pray over his back. He did, and all of a sudden the pain left; and he was able touch the ground, which he hadn't been able to do in fifteen plus years.

A woman with a broken wrist, that was on her way to have a surgical rod put in her hand. I prayed for her and she went into the hospital, only to come back out about twenty minutes later. The wrist was completely normal. Talk about a bunch of tears on that one.

A fellow in ICU had liver cancer, and a pancreas, that was not functioning. I spent about an hour with him. He was incoherent, because of the massive doses of medication they were giving him. After prayer he sobered up, and accepted Christ. His blood sugar went, from off the charts to three-hundred. He had so much improvement, that the nurses brought him a Sprite. The following day, he released himself (not recommended). He called me, and has been doing awesome ever since.

At Wal-Mart, I saw a woman in a wheelchair. It turned out she was going to have a hip replacement the next day. I told her my testimony, held out my hand; and she got up and started prancing around her wheelchair. I said "Do ya think you need that surgery now?" She said, "No way, Thank You Jesus."

Thanksgiving Day a year ago, I had to go buy a laptop. While we were waiting, a woman came up in a wheelchair, her husband was with her. I gave her my testimony. He didn't look interested, and said he had to go get something. When he returned, she was up prancing around! He looked at me and she said "Tony prayed for me, but it is all Jesus!"

At a Little Caesar's Pizza, I walked in to get my fantastic, regular lunch of pizza. The young girl at the counter was working extremely hard with one arm, the other one was in a sling. There was no one behind me. I asked what happened. She said that she had cracked her elbow. I said "Well, I'm praying for you". She went to get in her religious stance, and I said, "A large cheese pizza, In Jesus Name" I said. "How's the pain", She looked at me with a weird gaze and said "Oh my gosh the pain is gone". I told her to move it around, but she said the therapist told her that if she moved it, she would cause nerve damage. I said okay, and turned around to see about eight people in a line. They started to ask me to pray for them.

The next day, I went back there, and she was, without the sling, moving both arms. She looked at me and said, "After you left, I took the sling off, and it was super good!"

Here is the reason I'm sharing these testimonies. This should be normal Christianity. As we go about our daily lives, when there is a person in need, we have the ability to minister to them. It doesn't take a Benny Hinn, Catherine Kuhleman, or the many other "anointed healers". It just takes a willing YOU! There was a time, that it was needed to bring attention to the fact, that Jesus already paid for our healing. Here is a less than normal "Joe", who has been a part of all this. My desire is to share, what The Lord gave to me freely at the Cross. These healings didn't happen at a church, with the Pastor praying for them. It happens at Wal-Mart, Little Caesars, and wherever we are.

At a parking lot, a seventy year old man, with a cane, was barely able to walk. We talked, and he told me about how there used to be tents. How he had been healed as a little boy, by a healing evangelist. He said "How I wish they still came here so I could be healed". I said, "You're a believer, right?" He said "Oh yes, sir". I said command your back and knees to be healed. With a little prompting, he bent over and touched the ground. Then right there in a parking lot, in tears, lifted up his arms, and started praising the Lord. He was off in his own little world, and I got to share that moment with him.

A seventy year old woman, and I didn't even know anything was wrong with her, was listening to my testimony, and the phone rings. It was a person needing prayer. I prayed for the person over the phone, hung up, and continued to tell her my testimony. She looked at me and said "I don't need to hear anymore". I said, "Oh, I'm sorry for bothering you." and she said, "Noooo, it isn't that; when you were praying over the phone, The Lord healed me! Amen!".

Please do not get me wrong, I'm not against healing evangelists, or guys like Oral Roberts, Smith Wigglesworth or the many others; we needed them. Now, we need Leaders who will equip the saints, and get them praying for others in their everyday lives! I'm happy to say that this is happening! Today, there are many ministries doing just that. Teaching in churches, and then sending people out. I applaud them! JGLM is one them, Royal Family International with Pete Cabrera Jr. is another one, Inside Out Training and Equipping School with Cheryl Fritz is another. Oh yeah, Millian Quinteros is another! Yeah! You guys go!

It would be irresponsible of me, if I didn't give you at least a little taste of how to get started in walking out divine healing, whether for yourself or for others. First and foremost, to be healed is a choice that many have stolen from them by irresponsible teaching. One, of those teachings, is the idea of Faith. Today, many preachers still say, "You don't have faith if you aren't healed", when someone isn't healed. This happened to me. That is a lie, from the pit of hell. I don't care who you are or what your beliefs are, "YOU HAVE the FAITH!"

> **Romans 12:2-4 King James Version (KJV)**
> **2** And be not conformed to this world: but be ye trans-formed by the renewing of your mind, that ye may prove what *is* that good, and acceptable, and perfect, will of God. **3** For I say, through the grace given unto me, to every man that is among you, not to think *of himself* more highly than he ought to think; but to think soberly, according as God hath dealt to every man the measure of faith.

> **2 Corinthians 4:12-14 King James Version (KJV)**
> **12** So then death worketh in us, but life in you. **13** We having the same spirit of faith, according as it is written, I believed, and therefore have I spoken; we also believe, and therefore speak; **14** knowing that he which raised up the Lord Jesus shall raise up us also by Jesus, and shall present *us* with you.

Each person has the faith; indeed the same Spirit of faith resides in us all. Who is the Spirit of Faith? The Holy Spirit. We can know that we each have the faith. It simply has to be empowered by the correct belief, and by confident expectation. Believe that you are healed and you are! It is that simple. That is empowered FAITH and it is seen! Faith is the substance of things hoped (confident expectation) for; the evidence of things not seen. Hope is unseen; faith empowered by expectation is seen. When you need a healing for yourself, or praying for another person, first you speak;

Matthew 17:19-20 New Living Translation (NLT)

19 Afterward the disciples asked Jesus privately, "Why couldn't we cast out that demon?"

20 "You don't have enough faith," Jesus told them. "I tell you the truth, if you had faith even as small as a mustard seed, you could say to this mountain, 'Move from here to there,' and it would move. Nothing would be impossible."

Say to the mountain, that means speak, use your voice, and tell it what to do. Sickness leave; done deal. When you truly expect it to happen, it does. Now, I want you to remember this was before the cross, and before the day of Pentecost. After God poured His spirit out on all flesh, as Paul stated, we all have THE measure of Faith now! Right belief fuels our confident expectation, and faith is seen, which is the manifestation of the healing.

What is the correct belief? The correct belief is, that Jesus paid for our healing at the cross. It is a free gift. We have only to believe, that we are healed, and then we are. Salvation and Healing are one in the same thing. It was paid for, at the same time, so what applies to Salvation, applies to healing. When we accept salvation, what do we do?

Romans 10:8-10 King James Version (KJV)

8 But what saith it? The word is nigh thee, *even* in thy mouth, and in thy heart: that is, the word of faith, which we preach; **9** that if thou shalt confess with thy mouth the Lord Jesus, and shalt believe in thine heart that God hath raised him from the dead, thou shalt be saved. **10** For with the heart man believeth unto righteousness; and with the mouth confession is made unto salvation.

The same is true with healing, confess with your mouth, and believe in your heart that you are healed. Then you are. The only reason we have to teach healing, is to un-teach all the teachings of men. If you believe truth; you get truth; if you believe a lie, you get the lie. Here is a scriptural example:

Numbers 21:8-10 King James Version (KJV)

8 And the Lord said unto Moses, Make thee a fiery serpent, and set it upon a pole: and it shall come to pass, that every one that is bitten, when he looketh upon it, shall live.
9 And Moses made a serpent of brass, and put it upon a pole, and it came to pass, that if a serpent had bitten any man, when he beheld the serpent of brass, he lived.

The Serpent of Brass is a shadow of Christ. The Jews only had to look at the serpent to be healed. We need only to look at the cross to be healed. By his stripes, you were healed. Healing is always open; it's already there. You have nothing to do, but believe only. Unforgiveness can't block your healing. We don't have to wait for God's timing (it was 2,000 years ago), The only thing that can block a healing is not believing, that it already happened two thousand years ago. If we believe a lie, we get the lie. We need only command it, and expect it to happen. As I stated, this is just a mouth watering morsel. In order to have it happen, we need only to do, what <u>unknowingly I did</u> on July 4, 2012; command the problem to be gone, and it leaves.

Matthew 21:22 King James Version (KJV)

22 And all things, whatsoever ye shall ask in prayer, believing, ye shall receive.

In other words, when you believe that you have received it; then you shall have it. When I pray for anyone, it starts as a normal conversation, then as a course of action. I might say something as simple as "Be healed". Then, I simply ask them how they are. I know it happened. All I'm doing is getting them to acknowledge it. People normally call this "an Act of Faith", that implies action on our part to receive our healing. The action was done 2,000 years ago. I simply want them to recognise the pain left, the part moved.....whatever the situation. You could call it confirmation of the healing.

A fourteen year old boy had never walked. He had been in a car wreck in his mother's womb, before birth. This accident left scar tissue on his brain. I prayed for him simply by saying "Get up and walk" and he did. Thank You Jesus. If you have childlike faith, you will see the Kingdom of God. Throw all the theology and excuses out the door, and simply command the sickness to leave. Then expect results, look for them, and you'll see it happen.

I want to leave you with this. It is The Lord's Will for you to be healed. I can scripturally prove this, and I can show you by my testimony, that this holds true. The declaration I made that Jesus would heal me...... no healing; being prayed for by the elders.......no healing; to which many people, including myself, came to the conclusion, that it wasn't God's Will for me to be healed. Think again! I am now healed!! Never ever give up! Always HOPE (confidently expect), the healing to manifest right now! If there isn't a one hundred percent miracle, look and expect for more subtle improvements, such as the pain going from a ten to and eight. Praise The Lord, then expect for more! Take it for granted that you have the faith. Focus on Believing correctly and creating HOPE / confident expectation in your heart is...deep down, not just thoughts in your brain. One way, to do this, is through listening to testimonies, because they stir up confident expectation.

Be HEALED IN JESUS NAME.
God Bless, there is more to come!

ABOUT THE AUTHOR

Tony Myers has appeared on *Healing Miracles TV* with Joan Able and the podcast *Heal the Sick* with Millian Quintaros. Myers is involved with numerous Christian ministries, including Inside Out Training and Equipping School, where he serves as a host trainer.

Myers is available to provide personal testimony, teach on healing, or pray for the sick. Find Myers online at www.tonybelieves.com. Or contact him via e-mail at TonyJustBelieves@gmail.com.

Myers lives with his wife, Debra, near Cumberland National Park.

99904395R00039

Made in the USA
Columbia, SC
13 July 2018